MERIDIAN MIDDLE SCHOOL
2195 Brandywyn Lane
Buffalo Grove, IL 60089

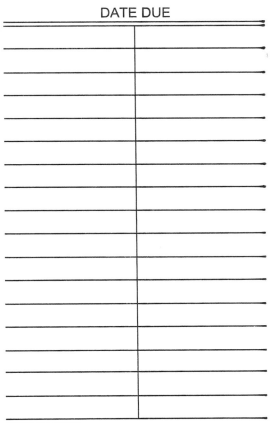

DATE DUE

DEMCO, INC. 38-2931

Endurance & Cardio Training

An Integrated Life of Fitness

Core Workouts

Cross-Training

Eating Right & Additional Supplements for Fitness

Endurance & Cardio Training

Exercise for Physical & Mental Health

Flexibility & Agility

Sports & Fitness

Step Aerobics & Aerobic Dance

Weightlifting & Strength Building

Yoga & Pilates

An Integrated Life of Fitness

Endurance & Cardio Training

Z.B. HILL

Mason Crest

Mason Crest
450 Parkway Drive, Suite D
Broomall, PA 19008
www.masoncrest.com

Printed and bound in the United States of America.

First printing
9 8 7 6 5 4 3 2 1

Series ISBN: 978-1-4222-3156-2
Hardcover ISBN: 978-1-4222-3160-9
Paperback ISBN: 978-1-4222-3198-2
ebook ISBN: 978-1-4222-8698-2

Cataloging-in-Publication Data on file with the Library of Congress.

CONTENTS

KEY ICONS TO LOOK FOR:

 Text-Dependent Questions: These questions send the reader back to the text for more careful attention to the evidence presented there.

 Words to Understand: These words with their easy-to-understand definitions will increase the reader's understanding of the text, while building vocabulary skills.

 Series Glossary of Key Terms: This back-of-the book glossary contains terminology used throughout this series. Words found here increase the reader's ability to read and comprehend higher-level books and articles in this field.

 Research Projects: Readers are pointed toward areas of further inquiry connected to each chapter. Suggestions are provided for projects that encourage deeper research and analysis.

 Sidebars: This boxed material within the main text allows readers to build knowledge, gain insights, explore possibilities, and broaden their perspectives by weaving together additional information to provide realistic and holistic perspectives.

INTRODUCTION

Choosing fitness as a priority in your life is one of the smartest decisions you can make! This series of books will give you the tools you need to understand how your decisions about eating, sleeping, and physical activity can affect your health now and in the future.

And speaking of the future: YOU are the future of our world. We who are older are depending on you to build something wonderful—and we, as lifelong advocates of good nutrition and physical activity, want the best for you throughout your whole life.

Our hope in these books is to support and guide you to instill healthy behaviors beginning today. You are in a unique position to adopt healthy habits that will guide you toward better health right now and avoid health-related problems as an adult.

You have the power of choice today. We recognize that it's a very busy world filled with overwhelming choices that sometimes get in the way of you making wise decisions when choosing food or in being active. But no previous training or skills are needed to put this material into practice right away.

We want you to have fun and build your confidence as you read these books. Your self-esteem will increase. LEARN, EXPLORE, and DIS-COVER, using the books as your very own personal guide. A tremendous amount of research over the past thirty years has proven that the quality of your health and life will depend on the decisions you make today that affect your body, mind, and inner self.

You are an individual, liking different foods, doing different things, having different interests, and growing up in different families. But you are not alone as you face these vital decisions in your life. Those of us in the fitness professions are working hard to get healthier foods into your schools; to make sure you have an opportunity to be physically active on a regular basis; to ensure that walking and biking are encouraged in your communities; and to build communities where healthy, affordable foods can be purchased close to home. We're doing all we can to support you. We've got your back!

Moving step by step to healthier eating habits and increasing physical activity requires change. Change happens in small steps, so be patient with yourself. Change takes time. But get started *now*.

Lead an "action-packed" life! Your whole body will thank you by becoming stronger and healthier. You can look and do your best. You'll feel good. You'll have more energy. You'll reap the benefits of smart lifestyle choices for a healthier future so you can achieve what's important to you.

Choose to become the best you can be!

—Diana H. Hart, President
National Association for Health and Fitness

Words to Understand

tissue: A certain type of material in your body, made up of cells, that does a certain job.

nutrients: Substances that you need to take into your body for it to work correctly.

contracts: Squeezes or gets smaller.

documented: Recorded or supported by information.

Chapter One

WHAT IS ENDURANCE?

Your body has amazing powers. Think about it. It moves. It takes in food and turns it into energy. It breathes in oxygen and sends it to each cell in your body. It grows. It is able to do all kinds of work.

But you can decide to make your body even more amazing by choosing to exercise regularly. Exercise improves your body's ability to do all the amazing things it's doing already. Exercise makes your body stronger, so that it can work harder—and longer. Being able to exercise longer is called endurance.

In the same way you can train your muscles to lift more weight, cardio workouts can help your endurance over time.

Endurance & Cardio Training

BODY SYSTEMS AND ENDURANCE

The human body is made up of many small parts that work together as a whole, starting with microscopic cells. These building blocks of life that cannot be seen without a microscope connect to form different types of *tissue*. That tissue makes up organs, and those organs make up body systems. The human body has several body systems that all work together to make sure the body functions as it should.

The respiratory system makes sure the body has the oxygen it needs, while the digestive system takes care of absorbing food and water. The musculoskeletal system is in charge of physical movement, and the nervous system allows us to feel, see, and think. Each body system has its role to play; if one body system is not used regularly, it will start to become weaker over time.

All body systems need to be exercised regularly, whether that means working out or eating the right type of foods. Lifting heavy objects for a long period of time is one way to strengthen the muscles in your arms and legs. The more you exercise these muscles, the more weight they will be able to lift. Over time, you will be able to lift more weight and hold it up for more time than ever before. When you can use the same group of muscles without it getting tired, that's endurance!

Every muscle in the human body needs to be exercised to stay healthy. It is easy to see the results from exercising skeletal muscles. These muscles will start to grow in size within just a few weeks of regular exercise. However, one of the most important muscles in the human body cannot be seen: the heart. This muscle also needs to be exercised, but the exercises use to strengthen this muscle are very different from the ones used to strengthen the arms and legs.

Muscle and cardiovascular endurance are just two of the five ingredients of physical fitness. The other three are muscle strength, flexibility, and body composition. All these components are part of a healthy fitness program.

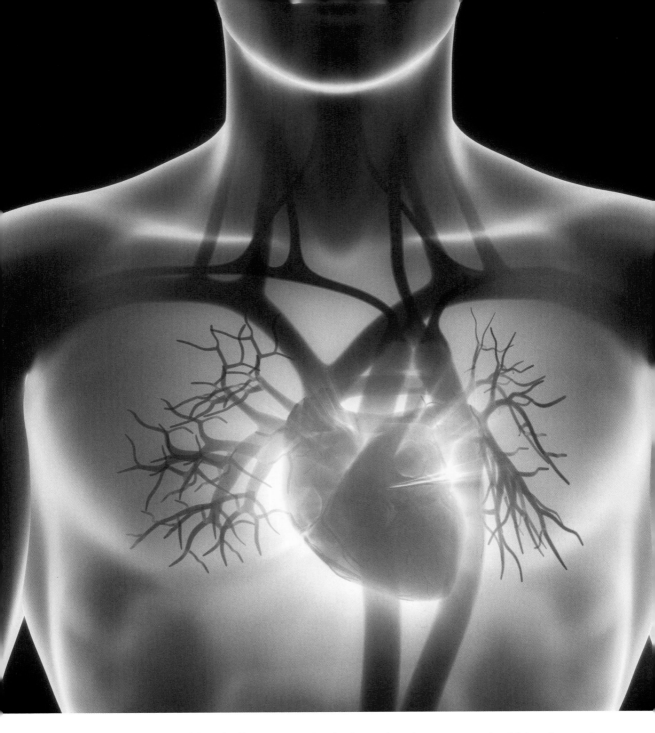

Your heart pumps blood all over your body through a huge network of blood vessels.

Endurance & Cardio Training

THE CARDIOVASCULAR SYSTEM

The cardiovascular system, responsible for cardiovascular endurance, is made up of the heart, blood vessels, and blood. At the center of the cardiovascular system is the heart. This organ is responsible for delivering *nutrients* and oxygen to every single living cell.

Cells need oxygen to survive. Cells that do not receive oxygen will start to die within a matter of minutes! The only way your cells can get oxygen is by your lungs breathing it in. Inhaled air enters the lungs, where the oxygen is absorbed into the blood within little air sacks known as alveoli. From there, the blood carries the oxygen on to the heart, and your heart makes sure it gets pumped out to the rest of your body.

Blood makes its way through a network of vessels, starting with large powerful arteries and ending with small, cell-thin capillaries. The blood cells remain in the bloodstream, while the oxygen and nutrients they were carrying are absorbed into cells along the way. All of this occurs at a microscopic level and cannot be seen with the naked human eye. After the necessary substances are brought to the cells, the blood travels back to the heart through the veins. From there, the process starts all over again.

Cardio exercise improves your health in many different ways, including your breathing, your weight, and your endurance.

Endurance & Cardio Training

The heart is made up of cardiac muscle, a special type of muscle only found in the heart. Cardiac muscle is unique in that it never stops working for as long as you are alive! When you're resting, not exercising, your heart **contracts** about sixty to one hundred times per minute as it pushes blood through every vessel in your body. This constant pushing is what makes your heartbeat. The amount of times a heart contracts in a minute is known as a pulse rate.

CARDIOVASCULAR ENDURANCE

Exercising causes a chain reaction in the human body. A body that is exerting itself requires more nutrients and oxygen than a body at rest. The heart will speed up to increase the rate of nutrient delivery to meet the needs of a working body, but the heart will not be able to keep beating that fast forever. It will get tired and eventually need to take a break. At the same time, the rate of respiration must also increase to accommodate the faster heart rate.

Regular exercise is necessary to keep any muscle healthy, and the cardiac muscles that make up the heart are no exception. Cardiovascular endurance is the ability for a human being to remain active for a long period of time without needing to rest. A person who can run 5 miles without stopping has a lot of cardiovascular endurance, while a person who can barely jog 500 feet has very little endurance.

Endurance can be increased through a number of effective physical exercises, but exercise alone will not make a heart healthy and strong. Eating right, sleeping enough, and remaining stress free are three important ways to prepare the body for cardiovascular training.

OTHER BENEFITS OF ENDURANCE

Being able to exercise for a long time without stopping is just one of the benefits of having good cardiovascular endurance. Some cardiovascular exercises are connected to metabolism—how quickly food and nutrients pass through the human body. Physically active bodies require

Even if you're just starting to work out, exercise can change your mood, help you sleep better at night, and make you feel better about yourself.

more energy than inactive ones. Training often forces the body to use energy faster, thus increasing metabolism speed.

This means that people who exercise regularly will have an easier time losing weight or staying fit because a lot of the energy taken into their bodies through food is used in the process of exercising. Energy obtained from food is measured in calories. One calorie in food is equal to the amount of energy needed to raise the temperature of one kilogram of water by one degree Celsius.

Physically fit people who say they are burning a lot of calories are actually saying they use a lot of energy while exercising. Food can be measured in calories—the amount of energy it provides the body. Health experts suggest that the average adult take in 2,000 calories per day. However, people who exercise frequently consume more calories because they are burning more calories in the process of exercising.

Regular exercise is also connected to feeling more energetic and happy, and there is a **documented** scientific reason for this. The reason has to do with hormones. Hormones are special chemicals your body makes and then releases directly into the bloodstream. These chemicals affect the body in different ways. Certain hormones are released during exercise, and each of these hormones serves a different purpose.

Adrenaline is released by the adrenal gland, and it causes the body to feel energized. People under the effects of adrenaline may feel stronger than usual. Adrenaline is not just released when a person is exercising, though. The chemical is also released when a person is afraid. This hormone is meant to help a person in a difficult situation have the energy to get through it.

Endorphins are what make a person feel good during and after exercise. Like adrenaline, endorphins are released during a number of situations. The pituitary gland releases endorphins when a person is in pain or excited, making the experience easier.

Adrenaline, endorphins, dopamine, and serotonin are all released during cardiovascular exercises. These feel-good hormones improve the

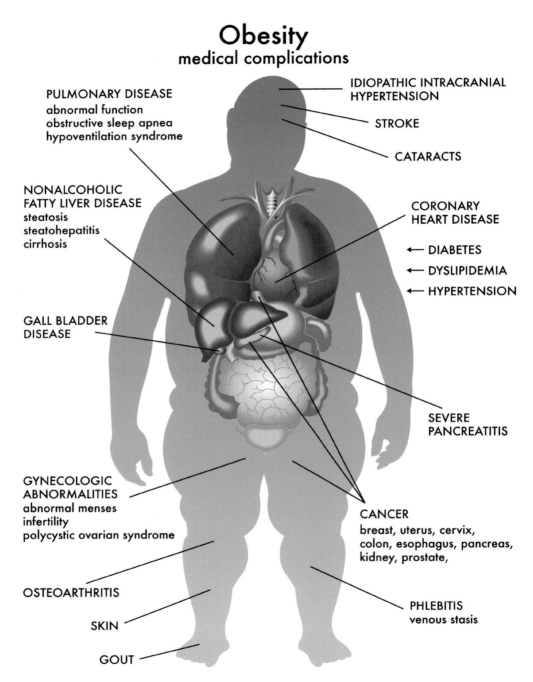

Obesity
medical complications

IDIOPATHIC INTRACRANIAL HYPERTENSION

STROKE

CATARACTS

PULMONARY DISEASE
abnormal function
obstructive sleep apnea
hypoventilation syndrome

NONALCOHOLIC FATTY LIVER DISEASE
steatosis
steatohepatitis
cirrhosis

CORONARY HEART DISEASE

← **DIABETES**

← **DYSLIPIDEMIA**

← **HYPERTENSION**

GALL BLADDER DISEASE

SEVERE PANCREATITIS

GYNECOLOGIC ABNORMALITIES
abnormal menses
infertility
polycystic ovarian syndrome

CANCER
breast, uterus, cervix,
colon, esophagus, pancreas,
kidney, prostate,

OSTEOARTHRITIS

SKIN

GOUT

PHLEBITIS
venous stasis

Lack of exercise can contribute to overweight and obesity, which can lead to a huge number of health issues.

Exercising regularly can help you have more energy than people who don't get enough physical activity.

overall mood and mental health of a person who exercises—and the effects are immediate! These hormones have been found in the blood stream after a workout as short as ten to fifteen minutes.

EFFECTS OF NOT EXERCISING

Just like there are positive effects from exercising, there are also negative effects from not exercising. One study estimates that about 250,000 deaths per year in the United States are caused by a lack of regular physical exercise. A person who does not exercise is much more likely to develop high blood pressure, heart disease, and diabetes than a person who exercises regularly.

What Is Endurance?

Using the Internet, research the five components of physical fitness. How are they similar, and how are they different? Explain why it is important to train each one. What would happen if you neglected to train cardiovascular endurance and chose to only train muscle strength instead?

Blood pressure is an important measurement having to do with the cardiovascular system. The exact measurement consists of two values: the blood pressure when the heart contracts, and the blood pressure when the heart is at rest. The blood pressure will naturally rise when a person is stressed or exercising, but it should never remain high for long.

Having high blood pressure is dangerous because it causes the heart to work harder than it should have to. A stressed heart is never given time to rest, and the pulse rate of a strained heart could stay elevated even when the body is not doing anything overly difficult. This means that people with high blood pressure are more likely to develop heart disease.

People who are overweight, smoke tobacco, or have high cholesterol are the most likely to have high blood pressure on a regular basis. One of the long-term effects of high blood pressure is hardening of the arteries. This occurs when certain waste products, such as cholesterol, get stuck inside artery walls.

Over time, high blood pressure can be deadly and even lead to heart disease. A heart that has been stressed for far too long may eventually stop working entirely during a heart attack. Sometimes, a heart

Text-Dependent Questions

1. What are the five components of physical fitness? Which component will be covered in this book?
2. What type of muscle is the heart made out of, and what makes that type of muscle unique?
3. What is cardiovascular endurance as defined by the author?
4. How will exercising regularly increase your metabolism? Explain.
5. Name two hormones that are released during and after cardiovascular exercise. What effects do they have on the body?
6. What is high blood pressure and why is it dangerous?

may start beating again on its own, but a lot of the time, it needs to be pushed back to the right rhythm through medical assistance.

The good news is—you can fix all the problems caused by not exercising by following a regular exercise plan, eating right, and paying attention to your body's needs. A person with a healthy heart might easily live to be over a hundred years old—and all it takes is at least thirty minutes of exercise each day!

Words to Understand

stamina: The ability to exercise for a long time.
neuroscientists: Scientists who study the brain and nervous system.
depression: A psychological condition where you feel sad and hopeless for a long time.

Chapter Two

HOW DOES CARDIO TRAINING HELP YOU BUILD ENDURANCE?

The only way to increase cardiovascular endurance is by exercising it. Aerobic—or cardio—training is a group of exercises that aim to work out the heart and lungs. Aerobic literally means "requiring air," as a person doing aerobic exercises will be breathing a lot while doing the training. The opposite of aerobic exercises are anaerobic. These involve strength training of the muscles and short-distance running, or sprinting.

Biking is a great example of cardio exercise, whether done outside or in a gym.

Endurance & Cardio Training

Make Connections

People who exercise correctly are reported to recover faster from injuries than those who do not exercise at all. Studies have proven that people who are physically fit have a stronger immune system and are 60 to 90 percent less likely to get the common cold. People who exercise regularly will quickly recover from the fatigue following a workout session if they are exercising correctly, as well.

Some ways to increase recovery rate (how quickly your body goes back to its normal functioning when resting) after a workout is by drinking plenty of water, eating right, stretching before and after a workout, sleeping well, and taking time to rest. Some experts also suggest meditating, as it will help keep the mind free of stress and irritation.

Cardio exercises are entirely about building *stamina* and endurance. Long-distance running, bicycling, and swimming are three common examples of cardio exercise. Aerobic exercises are not as intense as other workouts, but they do need to be done on a regular basis to see any real results. Exercising several days a week is a very important part of keeping the heart and lungs healthy and strong.

The exact amount of time each person should work out will vary. It is best to start off slow so that you can build up endurance as you go. Following a workout plan is a very good idea because it will ensure that you don't work yourself too hard or get hurt in the process. Using a schedule is also an effective way to stay on track and keep your mind on the long-term goal of a healthier body!

Patience is key when it comes to cardio training. It is possible that you won't feel any effects from the training until weeks after you start. Experienced runners have said that it takes at least ten days to feel any of the positive effects from working out, but not everyone is the same.

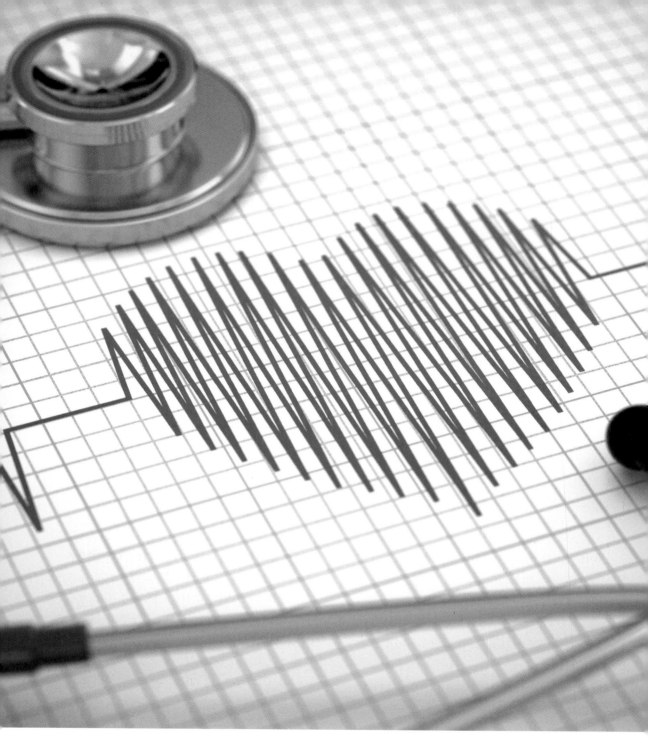

Cardio training helps your circulatory system's health, including reducing the risk of heart disease and high blood pressure.

Endurance & Cardio Training

The initial benefits of working out could come sooner or later, but the most important lesson to keep in mind is that it will eventually happen.

The main goal of cardio training is to improve cardiovascular endurance, but there are plenty of other added effects too. Regular exercise and cardio activity changes the way the whole body works, and only for the better!

CHANGES IN THE BODY

Regular cardio training changes the body in a number of ways, starting with the heart. The heart muscles will grow larger and stronger as they are pushed beyond what they are used to. This improves the heart's ability to pump blood faster and with less effort when it is needed.

Another added effect is a reduced pulse rate when the heart is at rest. Cardio training will also keep blood pressure low during rest, as well as exercise. Lower blood pressure and pulse rate means the heart is working less and is less likely to become diseased or damaged.

Incoming oxygen will be easier for your body's cells to get, as the lungs and respiratory system will grow thicker and stronger with repeated use. Individuals just starting cardio training may feel winded when they are done exercising, but after a few weeks, they will end

Cardio exercises like swimming or running have a huge effect your lungs, helping you breathe deeper and get more oxygen to your blood, allowing you to work out more.

28   Endurance & Cardio Training

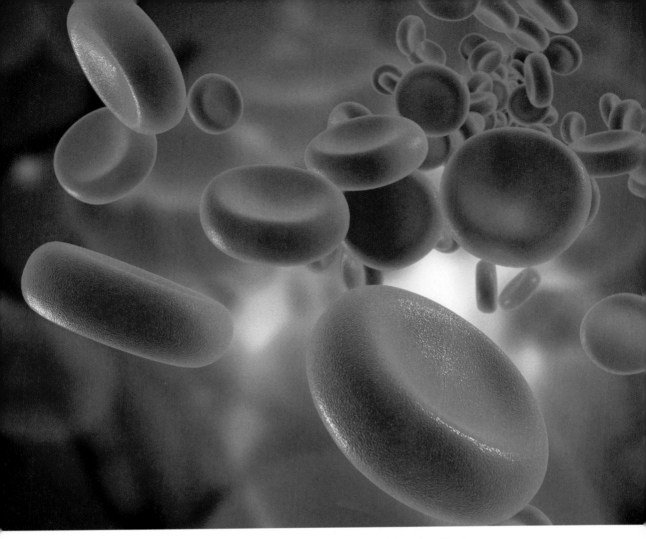

Cardio exercise changes your body right down to your blood cells. Running, swimming, biking, and other cardio exercise increase the number of red blood cells, bringing more oxygen to your muscles.

their workout without feeling tired or out of breath. Their lungs will be used to the strain of repeated use.

The circulatory system greatly benefits from cardio exercise. Red blood cells within the blood stream and the oxygen they carry increase in number through repeated aerobic training. More oxygen and nutrients reach every cell in the body, making every single cell in the body

How Does Cardio Training Help?   29

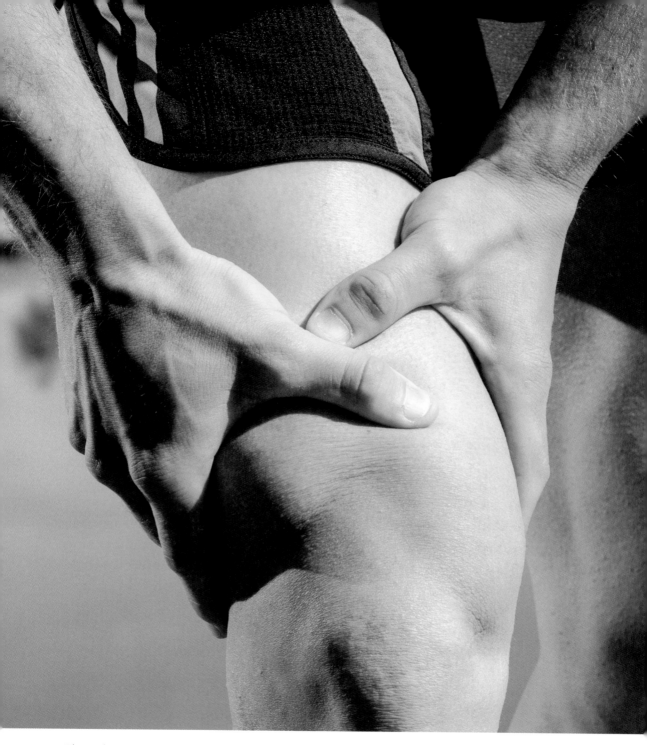

Though your muscles may hurt when you first start doing cardio, you'll soon adjust to the exercise.

Endurance & Cardio Training

Make Connections

Oxygen debt occurs when a muscle does not receive enough oxygen during a workout. The body's natural remedy to this is to produce lactic acid, but this is only a temporary solution. The oxygen the muscles were lacking during a workout must eventually be paid back. It can take several hours or days to pay back oxygen debt depending on the person's age, fitness, sex, and size. The length and intensity of the workout also affects the recovery time. Stretching immediately after a workout is one way to speed up the process.

healthier. The overall condition of the body is greatly improved as a result.

Cardiac muscle is not the only type of muscle that is strengthened by cardio exercises. The body contains two other types of muscle: skeletal and smooth muscle. Skeletal muscle gets its name from the fact that it is attached to bone. Smooth muscle is found inside many locations, including blood vessels, the stomach, and the intestines. Cardiac and skeletal muscles benefit from cardio exercise.

More than just your heart and lungs are getting a workout when you run, bicycle, or jog. Your legs, arms, and stomach muscles are working hard, too. This is why your legs might feel tired after walking too much, or your arms might hurt after a long swim. Over time, the skeletal muscles will get used to the exercise, just like the heart and lungs! Certain cardio exercises also help with muscle endurance.

One of the lesser-known benefits of cardio exercise is the effect it has on the human mind. One study performed by Swedish **neuroscientists** discovered that young men who use cardio training regularly tend to score higher on exams that test for intelligence than people who don't use cardio training. Other studies have been done to examine the link between heart disease and **depression**. People who do aerobics regularly are less likely to be depressed, while those with heart disease are more likely to be depressed.

MUSCLES

Cardio training causes a lot of interesting changes in the body, but the most obvious will be how easy it is to stay active after prolonged cardio training. The strengthening of the heart and lungs does more than just make it easier to breathe; the muscles being used during cardio exercises also receive more oxygen.

Muscles that are under a lot of strain need more oxygen than usual to work well during a cardio workout. A strong heart and lungs can supply enough oxygen to those who are physically fit for a long period of time, but people without a lot of endurance will eventually need to obtain their energy elsewhere. The body has a natural way of keeping muscles going even if they aren't receiving enough oxygen.

Lactic acid is a chemical produced within the human body that provides extra energy to tired muscles. It is made when glucose—a form of sugar—is broken down into a chemical called pyruvate, which is then formed into lactic acid. Unfortunately, there is a downside to lactic acid. It may accumulate faster than it can be removed, resulting in soreness after a workout is over.

You've probably heard that all athletes should spend time stretching both before and after a workout, but you may not know why. Stretching helps ease the pain associated with lactic acid buildup. It also allows the tired muscles to receive more oxygen, which was why the muscles needed the lactic acid in the first place.

Cardio training has amazing benefits for your mind and body. The next step is to find out how you can do it safely.

Words to Understand

circulation: The movement of blood between different parts of your body.

replenished: Filled up again; resupplied.

Chapter Three

EQUIPMENT & SAFETY FOR CARDIO TRAINING

You have a lot of options when it comes to cardio training. The easiest—and cheapest—way would be to run, but you could also use a bicycle or swim. Whether you want to exercise at home, outside, or in a pool, there is a cardio workout for you!

The effects these different workouts have on the skeletal muscles in your body will differ greatly, but they will all help with cardiovascular endurance. That's why a combination of multiple aerobic exercises may be the best choice for an overall workout. Doing the same thing every day could get very boring, but doing different exercises can make working out fun and exciting all over again!

EXERCISING OUTSIDE

One of the easiest ways to start cardiovascular training is by running. A few pieces of equipment might be used while running outside, but the most important involve safety and comfort. A good pair of running shoes is absolutely necessary for prolonged running, as uncomfortable feet can become sore and tired very quickly. Blisters are the last things any runner needs!

A runner should wear clothing appropriate for the weather, whether it is sweatpants, a jacket, or gloves. Runners who will be running during dawn or dusk should consider wearing a reflective vest. The vest will help drivers of motor vehicles see runners long before they get too close. Runners should always run against, or toward, traffic so they see drivers coming as well.

Having a running partner is helpful in a number of ways. The biggest reason is that it helps keep both runners on track. If one runner feels like giving up, the other runner can encourage the first runner to keep going. Motivation in numbers is one way to stick with an exercise plan. There will also be an extra set of eyes to watch what is happening and spot danger before it becomes a problem.

You may find that running with headphones helps the miles go past while you barely notice. Keep in mind, though, that for safety reasons, you should never have the music too loud. You need to be able to hear what is going on around you.

There are two more useful tools to consider using while running: a timer and a pedometer. Stopwatches are designed to time athletic progress down to the millisecond, and are great for runners who need to know how long it takes them to complete a certain distance. Stopwatches are also great for interval training, where you want to push yourself to your utmost for a period of time and then drop back to a slower pace. A pedometer, on the other hand, is useful for anyone just beginning training. A pedometer keeps track of how much distance a person has covered. It works by counting the steps a runner has taken and multiplying that by how long each step is. They are valuable tools for people who are sticking to a strict workout plan. They can motivate

Make Connections

All intense workouts should begin with a slow, steady warm-up. Athletes always drink a lot of water before any workout session. Don't eat a large meal right before a cardio workout—but don't try to do it on an empty stomach either. Try to eat a healthy meal a few hours before you plan to exercise. Taking a warm shower will warm up the body and muscles as well as open the pores. The function of sweat is to keep the body from overheating during activity, so having open pores will help with that process. All muscles should be thoroughly stretched before the workout begins. It is recommended to start any exercise with a less intense activity, such as jogging or walking to get the body ready for something harder.

you to keep running another five minutes so you complete that last mile—and they can also help prevent you from overworking yourself by going too far, causing unnecessary strain to your body.

There are many different types of pedometers. Some are meant to be used only for walking or counting daily steps. Others are designed for workouts, such as running or jogging. Some pedometers need to be attached directly to the body to count steps, while others can sense movement from your pocket.

Pedometers were once standalone devices that were only used for counting steps. Now, there are plenty of mp3 players and smartphones that have applications for workout tracking. Some of these applications will automatically track your progress and upload it to the Internet for all your friends to see as well. Posting athletic progress on social networking websites is one way friends can encourage each other to stay active and healthy.

Another outdoor option is bicycling. Bicyclists work out their heart, lungs, and leg muscles in the process of pedaling. The only downside is the arm muscles do not receive much of a workout because they aren't

Treadmills or stationary bikes are a great way to get a cardio workout inside.

Endurance & Cardio Training

being used. Buying a bicycle can be expensive, as even the simplest bikes are over $100. Many bike shops now offer a rental option, where you can rent a bike by the day.

INSIDE WORKOUTS

Exercising outside is not an option for everyone. Sometimes it will simply be too cold to go outside, or it may be raining too hard to go for a jog or a bike ride. Fortunately, there are a number of aerobic exercises that can be done inside your home or local gym. The equipment for each workout varies greatly.

The treadmill simulates running outside, but it can also be programmed to fit your exact needs. Some treadmills even ask for your height, weight, and fitness level. They can be set to go slow or fast, depending on your preference. Some of the more expensive treadmills can also tilt up to make it feel like you are running up a hill.

There are some advantages and disadvantages to using a treadmill. First, the distance it says you ran isn't always accurate. The amount of energy you need to exert to run is also not exactly the same as if you were running outside. The running belt helps move your feet, whereas you would normally have to lift your foot yourself if you were running on the ground.

A stationary bicycle is another indoor option. Like the treadmill, it can be programmed to your exact needs. The pedals can give as little or as much resistance as you want, making the workout only as difficult as you choose for it to be. Unlike a real bike ride, stationary biking does not have the element of surprise. There is no wind resistance or bumpiness on the ground to worry about.

The one downside to treadmills and stationary bicycles is that they are expensive. Even the cheapest treadmills and stationary bikes cost about $100. The more advanced ones can cost over $1,000! Gym memberships, on the other hand, work using a monthly fee. Members of a gym usually pay anywhere from $20 to $60 a month to use the equipment in the gym.

The final indoor aerobic option is step training, or moving up and

Swimming is an excellent way to build endurance, but safety must be a focus for swimmers looking to build endurance.

Endurance & Cardio Training

down steps. These steps could be a set of stairs in your house, or a small plastic step that you use at a gym. A cheap step costs around $30 and can be bought for home use as well. There is a whole set of exercises dedicated to step aerobics, complete with instructional DVDs, specific workout moves, and even a workout plan.

SWIMMING

Using a pool for cardio training is one of the most effective forms of aerobic exercise because the entire body is used while swimming. Water is denser than air, so moving through water requires more muscle effort than simply running or bicycling. Unfortunately, finding a place to swim can be difficult, depending on where you live.

Swimming requires one very important piece of equipment: a swimming pool! Some gyms and schools have swimming pools on the premises, but they may not be always available. Those who have access to a pool or lake at home will be able to use it regularly, but only if it is sunny and warm!

Some times of the year will not be ideal for outdoor swimming. Many pools need to be closed during the colder months. This is why swimming in an outdoor pool should never be the only aerobic exercise on an athlete's agenda. There should always be a backup plan in case swimming simply doesn't work out.

Certain safety measures should be taken while using a pool for cardio training. First, the person in the pool should know how to swim!

Lifeguards at public pools are absolutely necessary for safety reasons. If you are swimming at home, you should never go into the pool alone, no matter how well you swim. Make sure there is someone nearby to supervise. Accidents can happen. If you slip and knock yourself out, your swimming powers aren't going to do you any good.

AFTER A WORKOUT SESSION

Cooling down after an exercise session is almost as important as exercising in the first place. It ensures that all of your hard work does not go to waste. A lot of short-term changes happen to the body as it is exercising. The muscles heat up and are pumped full of extra oxygen and lactic acid to keep them going.

Immediately stopping after a workout is the worst thing you can do. Following a running session, you should take a few minutes to walk it off and calm down your body. Your lungs and heart are likely still working at a high intensity, and continuing to move will prevent the body from experiencing aches and pains later on.

After a few minutes of less intense activity, you should stretch out the whole body, especially the muscles that received the most intense

Research Project

This chapter mentions a number of different cardio exercises. Using the Internet or library, research at least three of the aerobic exercises mentioned and then pick the one you feel would be most effective for your own life. Explain why this activity would be better for your body and schedule than any of the other cardio exercises listed.

workout. The extra blood that was pumped into your muscles while you were working out always leaves the muscles after a workout is over. Muscles tend to contract as a result, and can feel very tight if they are not properly stretched.

By stretching muscles, you are preventing them from shrinking. They will grow bigger and stronger, instead. Stretching speeds up *circulation* in the tissues and joints surrounding the muscle and prevents lactic acid buildup, too. Athletes who stretch after an intense workout are able to prevent the soreness and stiffness associated with extensive cardio training.

Drinking water and eating food are just as important as stretching the body following a workout. The body will have used a lot of energy and water to keep the workout going, so all those fluids and energy need to be *replenished* somehow. Eating should be done no later than ninety minutes after a workout.

Eating not only gives the body more energy, but it also helps it heal. The muscles that were stressed during the cardio exercises can sometimes be a little injured in the process. Food will not only give the body energy to heal, but also the right chemicals to repair the muscles that were injured.

Now that you have some ideas as to how you can safely get involved with cardio training, it's time to make a plan!

Words to Understand

resilient: Able to recover or bounce back quickly.
professional: Doing something for a living.

Chapter Four

Making a Plan to Build Endurance with Cardio

Understanding the benefits of cardio training is a great start to becoming physically fit—but the only way to actually get there is by working out! Choosing an exercise plan is one of the most important steps to building cardiovascular endurance, and it should begin by picking which exercise works best for you.

MERIDIAN MIDDLE SCHOOL
2195 Brandywyn Lane
Buffalo Grove, IL 60089

Keeping track of the kind of exercise you're doing and how much you're doing is a big part of making a plan to build endurance through cardio.

The last chapter explored plenty of options for cardiovascular exercise. The equipment needed and the extra muscles it works out are what divide the options into categories. It is probably best to pick the exercise that seems easiest to start with, and move onto something more

Make Connections

Taking a break from training every few days is important, and so is taking regular short breaks during a workout! Just because your plan says you should spend thirty minutes on cardio exercises a day doesn't mean you should be working out the entire time. Athletes who use interval training alternate between a few minutes of active, intense cardio exercise and a few minutes of less intense movement. One example of interval training would be running for three minutes and then walking briskly for another three before running again.

difficult as time goes on. Jogging would be a great place to start for someone who is not used to exercising regularly.

Most recommended exercise plans include all aspects of physical fitness, from cardio training to muscle strength and flexibility exercises. Muscle strengthening exercises do not necessarily need to involve weights. Pull-ups, push-ups, and sit-ups are three strengthening exercises that can be done anywhere at any time.

Flexibility can be worked on through stretching. Many people who want to focus on flexibility choose to do yoga, as the poses used in yoga force the practitioners to flex in all sorts of ways they may not be used to. Lunges are another good method to work on flexibility.

EXERCISE DAYS

When making a lesson plan, remember your long-term goals. Do you just want to get in better shape, or do you want to lose weight too? Would you rather focus on building your endurance or increasing your

A balanced plan to build endurance includes strength training (such as push-ups) as well as cardio exercises.

Endurance & Cardio Training

If a runner is running 2 miles per day for five days a week, that would be a total of 10 miles per week. According to the Ten Percent Rule, runners should not increase their mileage more than 10 percent per week. In this example, the runner should only add on one mile to the next week, or 0.2 miles per day. Instead of running two miles per day, the runner will now run 2.2 miles per day.

muscle strength? A balanced beginner exercise plan will look something like this:

- Monday: 30 minutes of cardio training (5-minute warm-up and cool-down)
- Tuesday: 30 minutes of core strength training (5-minute cardio warm-up)
- Wednesday: Rest (light stretching and flexibility exercises)
- Thursday: 30 minutes of cardio training (5-minute warm-up and cool-down)
- Friday: 30 minutes of core strength training (5-minute cardio warm-up)
- Saturday: 30 minutes of cardio training (5-minute warm-up and cool-down)
- Sunday: Rest

This sample exercise plan focuses on cardio training for three days, strength training for two, and rest for another two. The first rest day can include some light flexibility exercises, but at least one rest day should contain absolutely no exercise whatsoever.

Taking a relaxing walk is a good way to stay active on your day off without pushing yourself too hard.

Endurance & Cardio Training

Taking days off is an important part of any workout plan, especially for people starting out.

Even the most experienced athletes must find time to rest. The human body is not a machine, and cannot go on forever without some recovery time. Muscles that are overworked can easily tear. Experts recommend at least one rest day per week, although athletes just starting out might want to take a little more. Athletes who absolutely do not want to stop working out can take slow walks on their rest days.

Making a Plan   51

Pushing yourself too hard can do much more harm than good. Make sure you're not doing more than you can and that you stick with small increases in your training.

Endurance & Cardio Training

WHEN TO INCREASE TRAINING

The goal of cardio training is to build endurance, so it is only a matter of time before you will want to increase the amount of training you will do. The most important rule is not to push yourself too hard. For example, if you don't feel comfortable running one mile a day yet, keep running a mile a day until you don't feel fatigued anymore. Only then should you increase the distance you run.

Every person is different, and so is the distance each person can comfortably run (or swim or bicycle). It can be hard to know how much is too much or too little when picking a new exercise plan. Fortunately, experienced runners have a general rule for people who are just starting cardio training: don't increase the distance of your workout by more than 10 percent a week. This is known as the Ten Percent Rule, and it is in place for two reasons.

The first reason for the Ten Percent Rule is safety. A body in training is still increasing in strength. Pushing yourself too far will only be bad for your body and could even result in injury. Your muscles will not be strong enough to handle much more than you are already doing, and they are more likely to become sore from any increase larger than 10 percent.

Trying to do too much in one week may also be discouraging and make you lose your focus altogether. Runners who feel overwhelmed by a new exercise plan are more likely to give up and quit exercising entirely. It is best to increase your mileage slowly so that you can feel confident about the steady progress you are making.

DON'T STOP

Just because you feel healthier doesn't mean you should stop exercising. It is easy to fall out of shape and eventually end up back at square one if you don't stick with your exercise plan. According to Edward Coyle, a professor at the University of Texas, the cardiovascular endurance

The most important part of sticking with an exercise plan is getting started each day. It may be tough, but getting your shoes on and getting out the door is a huge part of succeeding with your exercise goals.

Endurance & Cardio Training

Make Connections

Some individuals have certain health issues that may interfere with their ability to work out. One example is asthma, a condition that causes the openings of the lungs to swell under certain conditions. People who have asthma may find it difficult to breathe after prolonged physical activity. They should always consult a doctor before beginning cardio training.

you have worked up will "decline by half in about twelve days if you do nothing at all."

Even the most fit people will lose at least half of their overall training in just two weeks of not exercising, which is why it is important to continue to train, even if you don't train for the same amount of time as you once did. However, there will be weeks when you simply don't have the time to put into working out every day. Iñigo Mujika, the director of the USP Araba Sport Clinic in Spain, has a solution for this situation: "As long as you maintain high intensity, you can reduce volume by 60 to 80 percent, and that will help you preserve your training."

In other words, you can decrease the time you spend on working out each week, but only if you keep the workout intense. The heart, lungs, and skeletal muscles still need to be used at full intensity to keep the endurance they have built up. Exercising twice a week for thirty minutes or more is acceptable in this case. The only downside to this type of exercise is the fact that it will not increase endurance, only postpone a runner from losing it.

The only time you should take a complete break from training is if you are stressed, injured, or ill. Working out a body that is not at peak performance could only damage it more. The worst thing you can do to a body that is usually healthy is ignore the problems it has. Luckily, healthy bodies are **resilient**, and more likely to heal faster than bodies that are not.

SET GOALS

Setting up an exercise plan when you never have before can seem very daunting. Where do you start? The best way is to pick short-term goals and long-term goals. The short-term goals should be easy to obtain, such as sticking to an exercise schedule and trying not to skip a day. Your short-term goal can change from week to week as your experience and endurance increases.

Long-term goals give you something to reach for and strive toward in the distant future. One example of a realistic long-term goal is to participate in a race. Running and biking races happen all over the world, and they vary greatly by distance and experience. Some races only last for one mile, while others can last for thirty kilometers! Certain events host varying degrees of races for athletes of all abilities.

There are many benefits to participating in a race. First, you can see how much your training has changed your body. Second, you can

Text-Dependent Questions

1. Name three strength-training exercises that can be done in the home without any equipment whatsoever.
2. How many days of rest does the sample exercise plan suggest? Why are these rest days important?
3. What is the Ten Percent Rule and why is it so important?
4. What will happen if you stop exercising completely for two weeks?
5. When is the only time a person should stop working out completely?
6. What is one long-term goal suggested by the author?

compare yourself to the other athletes around you and feel good about what you have accomplished. You may even make some new athletic friends!

Finally, some races have prizes for people who finish within a certain amount of time, including medals or even cash rewards. Remember that not all people who participate in local races are **professional** athletes. Many are everyday people just trying to stay in shape and have fun while doing it. In fact, they could be you!

FIND OUT MORE

In Books

Bounds, Laura, Kirsten Brekken Shea, Dottiedee Agnor, and Gayden Darnell. *Health & Fitness: A Guide to a Healthy Lifestyle.* Dubuque, Iowa: Kendall Hunt, 2012.

Frederick, Shane. *Stamina Training for Teen Athletes: Exercises to Take Your Game to the Next Level.* North Mankato, Minn.: Capstone, 2012.

Greenfield, Ben. *Beyond Training: Mastering Endurance, Health, and Life.* Las Vegas, Nev.: Victory Belt Publishing, 2014.

Lancaster, Scott B., and Radu Teodorescu. *Athletic Fitness for Kids.* Champaign, Ill.: Human Kinetics, 2008.

Maffetone, Philip, and Mark Allen. *The Big Book of Endurance Training and Racing.* New York: Skyhorse, 2010.

Online

5 Key Components to Physical Fitness
www.abetterbodytraining.com/key_components_to_physical_fitness.html

Endurance Training for Sports
sportsmedicine.about.com/od/anatomyandphysiology/a/Endurance.htm

The Benefits of Physical Activity
www.hsph.harvard.edu/nutritionsource/staying-active-full-story

What's the Best Exercise Plan for Me?
www.helpguide.org/harvard/exercise-plan.htm

Fitness Training: Elements of a Well-Rounded Routine
www.mayoclinic.org/fitness-training/art-20044792

SERIES GLOSSARY OF KEY TERMS

abs: Short for abdominals. The muscles in the middle of your body, located over your stomach and intestines.

aerobic: A process by which energy is steadily released using oxygen. Aerobic exercise focuses on breathing and exercising for a long time.

anaerobic: When lots of energy is quickly released, without using oxygen. You can't do anaerobic exercises for a very long time.

balance: Your ability to stay steady and upright.

basal metabolic rate: How many calories your body burns naturally just by breathing and carrying out other body processes.

bodybuilding: Exercising specifically to get bigger, stronger muscles.

calories: The units of energy that your body uses. You get calories from food and you use them up when you exercise.

carbohydrates: The foods that your body gets most of its energy from. Common foods high in carbohydrates include sugars and grains.

cardiovascular system: Your heart and blood vessels.

circuit training: Rapidly switching from one exercise to another in a cycle. Circuit training helps build endurance in many different muscle groups.

circulatory system: The system of blood vessels in your body, which brings oxygen and nutrients to your cells and carries waste products away.

cool down: A gentle exercise that helps your body start to relax after a workout.

core: The muscles of your torso, including your abs and back muscles.

cross training: When an athlete trains for a sport she normally doesn't play, to exercise any muscle groups she might be weak in.

dehydration: When you don't have enough water in your body. When you exercise, you lose water by sweating, and it's important to replace it.

deltoids: The thick muscles covering your shoulder joint.

energy: The power your body needs to do things like move around and keep you alive.

endurance: The ability to keep going for a long time.

flexibility: How far you can bend, or how far your muscles can stretch.

glutes: Short for gluteals, the muscles in your buttocks.

hydration: Taking in more water to keep from getting dehydrated.

isometric: An exercise that you do without moving, by holding one position.

isotonic: An exercise you do by moving your muscles.

lactic acid: A chemical that builds up in your muscles after you exercise. It causes a burning feeling during anaerobic exercises.

lats: Short for latissimus dorsi, the large muscles along your back.

metabolism: How fast you digest food and burn energy.

muscle: The parts of your body that contract and expand to allow you to move.

nervous system: Made up of your brain, spinal cord, and nerves, which carry messages between your brain, spinal cord, and the rest of your body.

nutrition: The chemical parts of the food you eat that your body needs to survive and use energy.

obliques: The muscles to either side of your stomach, under your ribcage.

pecs: Short for pectorals, the muscles on your chest.

quads: Short for quadriceps, the large muscle on the front of your upper leg and thigh.

reps: How many times you repeat an anaerobic exercise in a row.

strength: The power of your muscles.

stretching: Pulling on your muscles to make them longer. Stretching before you exercise can keep you flexible and prevent injuries.

warm up: A light exercise you do before a workout to get your body ready for harder exercise.

weight training: Exercises that involve lifting heavy weights to increase your strength and endurance.

INDEX

lactic acid 31–33, 42–43, 61
lungs 13, 23, 25, 27–29, 31–33, 37, 42, 55

metabolism 15, 17, 21
microscope 11
muscle 10–11, 15, 20–21, 23, 27, 29–33, 35, 37, 41–43, 46–47, 49, 51, 53, 55
muscle endurance 31, 33
muscle strength 11, 20, 47, 49
musculoskeletal system 11

nervous system 11, 22
nutrients 8, 13, 15, 29

organs 11, 13
oxygen debt 31, 33

pedometer 36–37, 42
pulse rate 15, 20, 27
pyruvate 32

recovery 25, 31, 51

red blood cells 29
respiratory system 11, 27
running 23, 25, 28–29, 36–37, 39, 41–42, 47, 49, 53, 56

stamina 22, 25
stationary bicycle 39
stress 15, 25
stretching 25, 31, 33, 42–43, 47, 49
sweat 37
swimming 25, 28–29, 40–42

timer 36
tissue 8, 11, 43
treadmill 38–39

vein 13

walking 31, 37, 47

yoga 47

ABOUT THE AUTHOR AND THE CONSULTANT

Z.B. Hill is a an author and publicist living in Binghamton, New York. He has a special interest in education.

Diane H. Hart, Nationally Certified Fitness Professional and Health Specialist, has designed and implemented fitness and wellness programs for more than twenty years. She is a master member of the International Association of Fitness Professionals, and a health specialist for Blue Shield of Northeastern New York, HealthNow, and Palladian Health. In 2010, Diane was elected president of the National Association for Health and Fitness (NAHF), a nonprofit organization that exists to improve the quality of life for individuals in the United States through the promotion of physical fitness, sports, and healthy lifestyles. NAHF accomplishes this work by fostering and supporting state governors and state councils and coalitions that promote and encourage regular physical activity. NAHF is also the national sponsor of Employee Health and Fitness Month, the largest global workplace health and fitness event each May. American College of Sports Medicine (ACSM) has been a strategic partner with NAHF since 2009.

PICTURE CREDITS